Peace, Even Here

Finding Hope in the Midst of Loss
Because of Jesus

Kennedy Morris

Published by HoP Publishing.

Cover design by MoonStudio24_Tufan.

For my son, Parker, in heaven

and my daughter, Hollyn, on earth.

I love you both endlessly.

Introduction

If you've ever heard the words, "I can't imagine what you're going through," "I wouldn't be able to survive that," or "You're so strong," this devotional is for you, and I can relate.

I'm a 28-year-old mom of two. Our daughter, Hollyn, lives with my husband and me in our home here on earth, and our son, Parker, lives with our Lord and Savior in heaven. We lost our son when he was just three months old, and life has been completely different ever since.

I've changed so much since losing him. I love harder. I forgive easier. I understand that things can change in the blink of an eye. I don't take a single moment for granted.

If you've found yourself relating to what I've written, please know you're not alone.

I know how hard it can be to do anything in the days, weeks, and even months after loss. If all you can do is read, that is more than enough. If you feel like writing and reflecting, there are pages for that. If you can't or don't want to, that is okay, too.

At the beginning and the end of each devotion, I've included the Bible verse that inspired it. It was helpful to me to write the verses out, so there is space for you to do the same, if you would like.

I know there's nothing that can mend the hole in your heart, but I pray you're able to find and hold onto a little bit of peace.

Love,

Hollyn and Parker's Mama

Day 1

Hope, Somehow

Philippians 4:7 (ESV)

And the peace of God, which surpasses all understanding, will guide your hearts and your minds in Christ Jesus.

I once heard someone say, when your spouse dies, you're a widow. When your parents die, you're an orphan. But there is no word for when you lose your child.

Never in a million years did I think I would find myself in the category that has no name.

Before I can talk about grief, faith, or hope, I need to tell you about my son. His name was Parker. It still is. He was the sweetest baby boy and had the best giggle. The way his smile could light up a room is something I will never forget.

One Monday in March, my world went dark. Parker was found unresponsive at our home and rushed to the hospital by ambulance. They attempted extensive resuscitation. I watched a team of doctors and nurses work on my baby boy until I couldn't take it anymore.

That image is burned into my mind forever. I found myself waiting in a small room off the ER. After an excruciatingly long wait, the door slowly opened and the doctor walked in.

His demeanor said it all. I don't remember what he looked like, but I remember what his hands felt like when he grasped mine. His grip was firm, yet so gentle.

He squeezed my hands in his and said, "I am so sorry. We tried everything we could, and exhausted all options, but he didn't make it. I'm so sorry."

I couldn't make sense of what he said, but my heart knew. A warm tingling sensation spread throughout my entire body, starting at my head and ending at my toes. In that moment, it felt like the breath was sucked out of me.

A part of me died right there with my little boy. There are moments in life that divide everything into a before and after. This was mine.

My baby boy, who was part of every future I had ever imagined, was gone.

Those first few days were a blur. I barely ate. I barely slept. I asked God "why" more times than I could count.

At some point I found myself talking to God about Parker. I asked Him to hold him close. I asked Him to let Parker know how much I love him. I knew I couldn't speak to Parker directly, but talking to God about him brought me comfort. And more than that, it gave me something I didn't expect to feel so soon.

Hope.

What a powerful word in a time when death feels so heavy. The only reason I can say the word "hope" at all is because of Jesus.

Because I believe Parker is with Him.

Because I believe this is not the end of our story.

I have that hope. I know that Parker is with Jesus, and I will see him again one day.

That hope doesn't make me miss my little boy any less. It doesn't take away the ache or longing in my heart. It gives me something grief alone never could. Peace.

I remember a moment when I was overwhelmed with sadness and anger toward God. Then I remembered that

Parker is with Him. He is safe. He is whole. In a way I can't fully explain, peace washed over me.

A peace that surpassed all understanding.

In the eyes of the world, that doesn't make sense. Losing a child and having peace shouldn't go together. But that's what the hope of Jesus does.

It changes everything.

Write Out the Verse

Philippians 4:7

Day 2

Faith Like a Child

Matthew 18:1-4 (ESV)

At that time the disciples came to Jesus, saying, "Who is the greatest in the kingdom of heaven?" And calling to him a child, he put him in the midst of them and said, "Truly I say to you, unless you turn and become like children, you will never enter the kingdom of heaven."

In the hospital after we found out Parker was with Jesus, I remember asking my dad to go pick up my almost two-year-old daughter, Hollyn. I wanted to hold her close and tell her I loved her. I needed to hug her and feel her warmth and presence.

When Hollyn arrived at the hospital, she walked into the room in the ER where we were waiting, and when she saw me, her eyes lit up. She ran to me, and I scooped her up into the biggest hug I'd ever given her. I told her I loved her so much.

She realized everyone was crying and ran from person to person, pointing at them and exclaiming, "Sad!" We explained to her that Parker was not going to come home with us because he was visiting Jesus. We told her that we were very sad and that we would miss him very much.

After an hour or so, Hollyn was coloring with one of the Crisis Response Team members, perfectly content with the same joy she always exuded. In the middle of everything that had just happened, she was able to play. She was able to smile and she was able to make others smile. She knew something wasn't right and she could see our sadness, but she also trusted that she was being cared for.

I was so thankful for her in those moments. After reflecting on that day, I realized I learned so much from her. Just as she trusted us to still be there for her and to still care for her, I can trust God to still be there for me and to care for me, despite my circumstances. The world can be crumbling around me, but I can still have hope that God is there. He hasn't abandoned me.

I learned what having faith like a child means. I don't have all the answers. I don't have *any* of the answers. I might not ever understand why, but I can trust that I am still loved, still held, and still cared for by a loving Father in heaven.

Write Out the Verses

Matthew 18:1-4

Day 3

Trusting Anyway

Proverbs 3:5-6 (ESV)

Trust in the LORD with all your heart, and do not lean on your own understanding. In all your ways acknowledge him, and he will make straight your paths.

About one month before Parker passed away, he was dedicated to the Lord at our church. We chose the verses Proverbs 3:5-6.

I've always had a special place in my heart for those words. My grandma loves those verses and shared them with me when I was in high school. She gave me a visor clip with those verses engraved on it that I've kept in my car ever since. I've had three different cars since then and it's made its way to each one.

Each car represented a different season of my life, and in each season, those verses meant something different.

In the season of my 1999 Ford Taurus, trusting in God meant looking to Him for guidance about what I wanted to do with my life. At that time, I had no idea.

In the season of my 2021 Mitsubishi Mirage G4, trusting Him meant carrying me through a lot of hurt and sadness caused by different people in my life at the time.

However, those seasons will never compare to the season of my 2019 Kia Sorento - the car I got right after we had our first child and the car I had when Parker passed away. This car went from having one car seat, to two car seats, back to just one after Parker's death. But the visor clip stayed the same. About one week after Parker died, I was filling out an auto insurance application, and one of the questions stopped me in my tracks. "How many children live with you in your home?" How could I possibly type "1" when the answer should have been "2"? I abruptly closed out of that application on my phone because I could not bring myself to type "1". In this season, I found myself questioning that verse for the first time.

What happens when your own understanding fails?

What happens when you can't make sense of the why?

My own understanding had never really failed until my son died. I can't make sense of Parker's death and I don't think I ever will on this side of heaven. For the very first time, I had to let God take the lead in my life. My plans for our family completely crumbled. The future I dreamed of was gone. I had to look to God because I was completely broken. I gave up complete control of my life, and I wasn't afraid of anything anymore. My worst fear had already come to life. I *had* to rely on God. Although nothing about losing Parker makes sense to me, I'm choosing to trust Him anyway.

Write Out the Verses

Proverbs 3:5-6

Day 4

Even This

Romans 8:28 (ESV)

And we know that for those who love God all things work together for good, for those who are called according to his purpose.

After Parker's death, I went through the typical questions:

Why did this have to happen?

Why our family?

Why our baby?

I couldn't answer those questions and neither could anyone else. I'm wired to find the good in every situation, and for the first time in my life, I couldn't find a single thing that was good. Not one. Then I realized it wasn't my job to find the good in this situation. I could leave that part up to God.

Slowly, God began showing me glimpses of how Parker's death could be used for good by the way He's connected me with others. I was able to relate to so many other moms who had lost children, specifically babies. After a child passes, so many people say things such as, "I can't imagine what you're going through." These moms didn't have to imagine because they were living it. It was comforting talking to people who know what it's like because you don't have to try to explain the unexplainable.

Some of these moms were farther ahead in their journey than I, and others were only a week or two behind me. One of the moms I connected with had a similar story so we could relate, which ultimately led to praying for each other and our families.

Although I don't understand God's plan in this, I choose to believe something good will come out of it.

I don't know exactly where God's leading me, but I do know if I obey, He will bring good things out of this.

Write Out the Verse

Romans 8:28

Day 5

Because of Jesus

John 3:16 (ESV)

For God so loved the world, that he gave his only Son, that whoever believes in him should not perish but have eternal life.

What I've learned through Parker's story is something I've always believed but never had to cling to. Death is not the end of the story.

Because of Jesus, Parker is in paradise.

Because of Jesus, I have hope.

Because of Jesus, I will see my little baby again.

Because of Jesus, this is not the end of our story.

Parker passed away thirteen days before Easter. On Good Friday, I was thinking about how to put my grief into words. I found three words that summed it up well: homesick for heaven. There's a tug in my heart for Parker. I feel it strongly at times and less strongly at other times, but it hasn't gone away since the day I lost him.

Remembering where Parker is helps me cope with his loss, and on that Good Friday I was grateful for the sacrifice Jesus made on the cross. I still am. I can only imagine, but I think Good Friday in heaven would look something like this: People surrounding Jesus, overwhelmed with sheer gratitude and thankfulness for Him. There's no fear. Parker's there, giggling and smiling, and being loved by the King of Kings.

I am so thankful for the sacrifice Jesus made on the cross. He understands pain. He understands loss. Most importantly, he understands love. In the grand scheme of eternity, life here on earth is very short. Keeping that perspective helps me deal with the loss of my sweet baby, and I cling to the hope that I will see him again one day.

Parker got to spend his very first Easter in heaven!

The reason I can continue living this life, even after my baby died, is because God is love. He loved us so much that he gave us Jesus. Jesus gives us hope through what He did on the cross over 2,000 years ago. He died for

Parker. He died for me and He died for you. He rose from the dead, defeating death for all of us, so we can have eternal life with Him.

There will be pain in this life. There will be sadness. More importantly, there is hope.

Write Out the Verse

John 3:16

This Is Not the End

Although I've come to the end of this devotional, it is not the end of my story, or the end of yours. Grief is a journey filled with ups and downs, sadness and healing, questions and quiet moments of peace.

In some of my hardest moments, God met me through His word. I want to leave you with some verses that bring me comfort. I encourage you to open your Bible to look up each verse.

Joshua 1:9

Psalm 23:4

Isaiah 41:10

Matthew 5:4

Matthew 11:28

Romans 15:13

Hebrews 6:19

Revelation 21:4

My prayer for you is that you would feel God wrap His arms around you, that you would feel His love and His strength. I pray you remember the same hands that hold your little one are the hands that are holding you.

Reflection

www.ingramcontent.com/pod-product-compliance
Lightning Source LLC
LaVergne TN
LVHW090542110826
845146LV00003B/1233

* 9 7 9 8 2 3 4 0 8 4 6 4 4 *